FIND FENTON!

can YOU track down the world's most disobedient dog?

Martin Berry & Stuart Cooper

headline

CONTENTS

MISSING DOG

Name: Fenton
Breed: Labrador, long-haired
Colour: Black
Last seen: Richmond Park
Likes: Chasing deer, hiding
Dislikes: Leads, collars, being shouted at
Favourite song: *Don't Stop Me Now*
Favourite film: *The Hidden*
Is all of this really relevant?: Not really, no
Reward: I'll get back to you on that one

Have you seen this dog? One moment he was running around like a lunatic in Richmond Park, upsetting lots of people and a considerable number of deer. Now, not surprisingly, he has gone into hiding, concealing himself at some of London's most popular attractions and events. You can usually tell when he's around because of the trouble and chaos that accompany him. Can you find Fenton in the crowds? Hurry up before he turns the city into a dog's dinner.

TRACKS AND TRAILS

Like all animals – and especially naughty dogs – Fenton leaves signs of his presence wherever he goes. If you can find all of these things in each scene while you're looking for him, you must be as sharp as Sherlock and as eagle-eyed as an, erm, eagle.

Footprints

Fenton never usually likes to make a good impression but sometimes he can't help himself. You can always find his footprints – or if we're being pedantic, pawprints – in the places he visits. But they won't necessarily lead you to him; Fenton's far too clever for that.

Collar

Fenton has a collar but he casts it off whenever he can. You see, for him it's a symbol of repression, of our enslavement to the military-industrial-capitalist system. Yes that's right, Fenton's a bit of an anarchist. Plus he also finds it a bit too tight, even on the loosest setting.

Lead

As anyone knows a lead is essential for keeping a dog under control. But what must it be like to be forced to wear one? Try imagining you're a dog for a moment: *...hungry, must eat... doorbell, must bark... nice smell, must pi...* On second thoughts, don't do that. Suffice to say that Fenton hates his lead even more than his collar, and wishes he could lose it forever.

Stick

What's brown and sticky Part 1? Correct. As it's his only possession – or the only one he chose for himself – Fenton's stick has a special place in his heart. But it also makes him sad because he can't ask anyone to throw it for him – that would give him away. So if you find it, please pretend to throw it so he can pretend to fetch it.

Turd

What's brown and sticky Part 2? Correct again. There isn't a delicate way of putting this but Fenton likes to relieve himself on a regular basis. Being a dog he doesn't care where he leaves his turd and doesn't bother to clear it up. There isn't much more to say about it really, only that it's an example of what Dr McKeith might call 'the perfect chocolate whippy'.

Deer

When Fenton escaped from Richmond Park a deer escaped with him, and seems to turn up wherever Fenton appears. Is Fenton chasing him or is he chasing Fenton? Is he the HunTer or the HunTed? Nobody knows, but his name isn't Ted, it's Darren, and you'd better find him fast before someone gets hurt.

Richmond Park

Oh deer! A labrador has run riot in Richmond Park, sending rattled ruminants into the road and forcing cars into emergency stops. But things are slowly returning to normal. The joggers are jogging, the Tai Chi enthusiasts are Tai-ing their Chis and the Richmond Dog Walkers have come out in force to demonstrate proper pooch control. Meanwhile the cause of the mayhem has gone to ground. This is it, the start of our quest. Pack up your pooper scoopers, unleash your leashes – it's time to **FIND FENTON!**

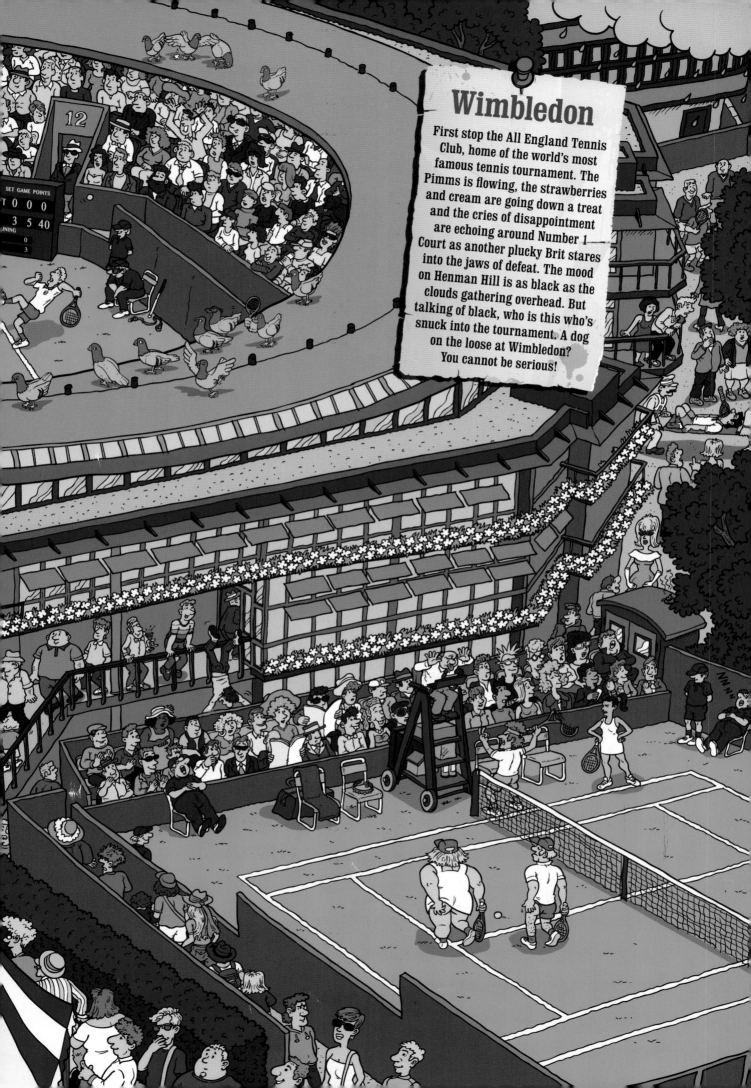

Wimbledon

First stop the All England Tennis Club, home of the world's most famous tennis tournament. The Pimms is flowing, the strawberries and cream are going down a treat and the cries of disappointment are echoing around Number 1 Court as another plucky Brit stares into the jaws of defeat. The mood on Henman Hill is as black as the clouds gathering overhead. But talking of black, who is this who's snuck into the tournament. A dog on the loose at Wimbledon? You cannot be serious!

SET GAME POINTS

12

The Boat Race

Except for during the two World Wars, the Oxford and Cambridge Boat Race has been held every year since 1856, when the students were much posher and could easily afford their tuition fees. Today, as they near the finish the boats are neck and neck and thousands are holding their breath, not because they care who wins (answer: either Oxford or Cambridge) but because a protestor is about to be scuppered. Somewhere amongst it all is Fenton, who has a First Class Hons. in Hiding.

Notting Hill Carnival

It's time to put on your sparkliest costume and shake your booty to the sound systems and steel bands of Europe's biggest street festival. The police are as chilled as their ice creams and some are even getting down and dirty with badass dance moves (well, more of a Tango Foxtrot). A rumour's going round of a special guest appearance by that crucial roots reggae band The Labradorz (feat. Fenton) but there's no sign of them yet.

The Proms

'Land of Hope and Glory,
Mother of the Free,
How shall we extol thee,
If a black dog we can't see?
Closer still and closer,
We must surely look;
Or we'll never manage,
To finish this blooming book.'

It's the Last Night of the Proms and the Promenaders are singin' along to Sir Eddie Elgar, and making sure that the sun never sets on the British Empire... alright, South Kensington. Fenton prefers Bach; but where is he Haydn?

THE PROMS

Buckingham Palace

'One is pleased to welcome you to one's annual garden party. One hopes you will have an enjoyable day, meeting one's family, some foreign dignitaries and a few ordinary people who have probably done something splendid. A small point to mention before one goes orf to mingle. Apparently one's party has been crashed by a black labrador. One was not amused to hear this, in fact one did not even titter. A Queen's ransom to whoever apprehends this intruder!'

Tate Modern

The Tate Modern houses one of the world's most important collections of contemporary art. Here you can marvel at the Matisses, be wowed by the Warhols, rave about the Rothkos and heave at the Hirsts. Today things are totally surreal as the paintings and sculptures have all come to life. Could this be something to do with that renowned Poop Artist Fenton? Yes he's in here somewhere, proudly displaying a work from his Brown Period — Giant Whippy Turd 2010.

St Pancras Station

For newly arrived Continentals St Pancras provides an impressive gateway to London and a chance to escape the football fans who look set to continue their punch-up on the platform. Maybe this announcement will distract them: 'Due to a technical fault there are some changes to the normal service. The train on Platform 8 is the 1840 from Dodge City; the train on Platform 5 is the 1940 Evacuation Express.' Yes, Fenton's here and things are going off the rails.

SUPPORT THE COO

EVEN ANGRIER BIRDS

FOLLOW US ON TWITTER

Trafalgar Sq.

Trafalgar Square

'England expects that every man will do his duty.' Stirring words, Lord Nelson, but you didn't expect that the duties of Englishmen would one day include fighting pitched battles with the police right under your stony nose. Yes, if you've got a point to make, this is the place to make it. Even the pigeons are protesting, probably about the feeding ban. But Fenton isn't seeking attention; like Nelson's right hand, he prefers to stay undercover.

London Zoo

Guy the Gorilla, Chi Chi the Panda, Goldie the Golden Eagle – London Zoo has been home to some of the world's best-loved animals. Its latest acquisition, Fenton the Labrador (*Canis richmondii*), is proving rather less popular. The Aquarium is flooded, there's a riot in the Reptile House and beasts are breaking out all over the place. The cause of the commotion is as slippery as a snake. Find him quickly before he makes a monkey out of you.

Camden Market

'Here we are in the urban jungle of Camden Town, in a clearing known as a market, where a host of exotic creatures are displaying a variety of fascinating behaviours. Some are here to gather food, some are looking for nest-building materials or ways of enhancing their plumage...' Sorry Sir David, I don't want to seem rude, but we're pretty busy right now, trying to find an escaped dog. He's a black labrador and the only behaviour he's interested in is of the naughty variety.

Leicester Square

'Mwah mwah, hello darling, are you looking forward to the film? Fenton's sooo adorable. There's a scene where he and Fentonia look into each other's eyes, sniff each other's bottoms and chase a deer into the sunset. Sooo moving.' Yes, our hero's fame has propelled him up onto the silver screen. All of his famous four-legged friends have been invited to the premiere, but our star must be suffering from opening-night nerves; he's nowhere to be seen.

Hamleys

It's time to go shopping at Hamleys for the latest toys. Top of the wishlist this year are the Mega-Pressure Super-Soaker with Laser-Dot Scope™ (batteries not included) and the Pool Princess Party Set with Pool Friends and Poolside Games™ (pool not included). Unfortunately, both are sold out, but something even more exciting has just arrived: a Fenton the Labrador with Easily Detachable Lead plus Collar, Stick, and Deer Prey-Buddy™ (all included). Hurry while stocks last!

Somerset House

And so to our final destination, Somerset House on the Strand, where every winter the courtyard is turned into an ice rink. In this magical setting Londoners can glide and spin and leap and dream that they are Torvill or Dean – in that split second before they crash onto the ice. But no-one cares because it'll soon be Christmas. A time to eat, drink, be merry, exchange gifts and celebrate the birth of our Lord – wait a minute; Fenton, is that you; come here! – Jesus Christ!

CHECKLISTS

If you've got this far you must have found Fenton and his pawprints, lead, collar, stick, turd and deer friend/enemy in every scene. You have, haven't you? Look at me... OK, I believe you. Now you've got to find this lot.

Richmond Park

- ☐ Robin Hood
- ☐ Bone
- ☐ Frisbee
- ☐ Dog weeing
- ☐ Man weeing
- ☐ Boy with scissors
- ☐ Doggie jumper
- ☐ Lazy cyclist
- ☐ Mountie
- ☐ Man on a lead

Wimbledon

- ☐ Bum scratchers
- ☐ Bottle of gin
- ☐ Broken racket
- ☐ Pigeon racket
- ☐ Racket accident
- ☐ Balcony accident
- ☐ Goofy couple
- ☐ Nude photographer
- ☐ Sleeping spectator
- ☐ Separated twins

The Boat Race

- ☐ Fry-up
- ☐ Pickpocket
- ☐ Mine
- ☐ Radio
- ☐ Periscope
- ☐ Gondolier
- ☐ Two lifebuoys
- ☐ Two sleepy students
- ☐ Pipe smoker
- ☐ Loud hailer

Notting Hill Carnival

- ☐ Skirt on fire
- ☐ Rasta pigeon
- ☐ Fruity hat
- ☐ Gold medallion
- ☐ Brown sauce
- ☐ Maracas
- ☐ Falling can
- ☐ Chicken
- ☐ Spider
- ☐ Bee

The Proms

- ☐ Adolf Hitler
- ☐ Jedward
- ☐ Susan Boyle
- ☐ Geri Halliwell
- ☐ Three knights
- ☐ Gio Compario
- ☐ Evil cellist
- ☐ Flag head
- ☐ Leek
- ☐ Rat

House of Commons

- ☐ Chicken
- ☐ Nose picker
- ☐ Ed Miliband
- ☐ Dave Cameron
- ☐ George Osborne
- ☐ William Hague
- ☐ Eric Pickles
- ☐ Guy Fawkes
- ☐ Conkers
- ☐ Hairdryer

Buckingham Palace

- ☐ Prince Harry
- ☐ Prince William
- ☐ Duchess of Cambridge
- ☐ Prince Charles
- ☐ Duchess of Cornwall
- ☐ Bruce Forsyth
- ☐ Shark
- ☐ Crown
- ☐ Pigeon in bearskin
- ☐ Squirty flower

Tate Modern

- [ ] Salvador Dali
- [ ] Toulouse-Lautrec
- [ ] Andy Warhol
- [ ] Damien Hirst
- [ ] Tracey Emin
- [ ] Banksy
- [ ] Boy weeing
- [ ] Aussie
- [ ] Broom
- [ ] Fisherman

St Pancras Station

- [ ] Pigeon wearing beret
- [ ] Two trainspotters
- [ ] Man dressed as nun
- [ ] Lovers embracing
- [ ] Lovers about to embrace
- [ ] Two hobos
- [ ] Four Germans
- [ ] Two Spaniards
- [ ] Three porters
- [ ] Six Native Americans

Trafalgar Square

- [ ] Princess Beatrice
- [ ] Abseiler
- [ ] Boat
- [ ] Guitar
- [ ] Ice cream
- [ ] Angry driver
- [ ] Art thieves
- [ ] Swan
- [ ] Umbrella attack
- [ ] Pirate

London Zoo

- [ ] Gorilla playing drums
- [ ] Zebra crossing
- [ ] Caged humans
- [ ] Boomerang
- [ ] Two bats
- [ ] Two big game hunters
- [ ] Eight disguised penguins
- [ ] Beaver
- [ ] Dracula
- [ ] Snorkeler

Camden Market

- [ ] Three generations of punks
- [ ] Punk pigeons
- [ ] Fenton shirts
- [ ] Teddy bear
- [ ] Ironing sculpture
- [ ] Living sculptures
- [ ] Union Jack
- [ ] Peace symbol
- [ ] Old telephone
- [ ] Tomato ketchup

Unolympic Games

- [ ] Speared pigeon
- [ ] Sandcastle
- [ ] Cup of tea
- [ ] Hotdog
- [ ] Fish
- [ ] Tortoise
- [ ] Knitter
- [ ] Wig
- [ ] Egg
- [ ] Snail

Leicester Square

- [ ] Doctor Who and K9
- [ ] Jean and Uggie
- [ ] Paris and Mugsy
- [ ] Churchill
- [ ] Lassie
- [ ] Toto
- [ ] Hound of the Baskervilles
- [ ] Snoop Dogg
- [ ] Dog taking photos
- [ ] Two pigeons wearing bowties

Hamleys

- [ ] Teddy in distress
- [ ] Drink spillage
- [ ] Voodoo doll
- [ ] Slinky girl
- [ ] Rocking horse poo
- [ ] Ball-shaped head
- [ ] Bowl on head
- [ ] Royal family
- [ ] Burger
- [ ] Alien abduction

Somerset House

- [ ] Torvill and Dean
- [ ] Scottish pants
- [ ] Michael Jackson
- [ ] Skating sticks
- [ ] Caveman
- [ ] Santa Claus
- [ ] Skating Germans
- [ ] Snowman skater
- [ ] Snowman spectator
- [ ] Flying granny

Acknowledgements

Martin Berry would like to thank Benjamin Fleming-Dufour for his assistance with colouring the artwork.

Stuart Cooper would like to thank Ali and Jake Goodyear, without whom this book would have been impossible; Viral Spiral for helping to seal the deal; Sarah Emsley, Richard Roper, Patrick Insole and the rest of the wonderful team at Headline; Andrew Evenden at Hamleys; Matt Nicholls at the BBC; Pamela Gillis Management; Bob Baker; Wendy Instrell; Alex Juras; and last but not least my nearest and dearest: Liz Payne and Ben and Sophie Cooper for their brilliant ideas and support, and for agreeing to have another dog in the house for the best part of a year.

ViralSpiral

Produced in association with Viral Spiral
www.viralspiralgroup.com

First published in 2012
by HEADLINE PUBLISHING GROUP

1

Cataloguing in Publication Data is available from the British Library

ISBN 978 0 7553 6399 5

Illustrations by Martin Berry martinberryart.co.uk
Text by Stuart Cooper

Printed and bound in Italy by
Rotolito Lombarda S.p.A

HEADLINE PUBLISHING GROUP
An Hachette UK Company
338 Euston Road
London NW1 3BH

www.headline.co.uk
www.hachette.co.uk

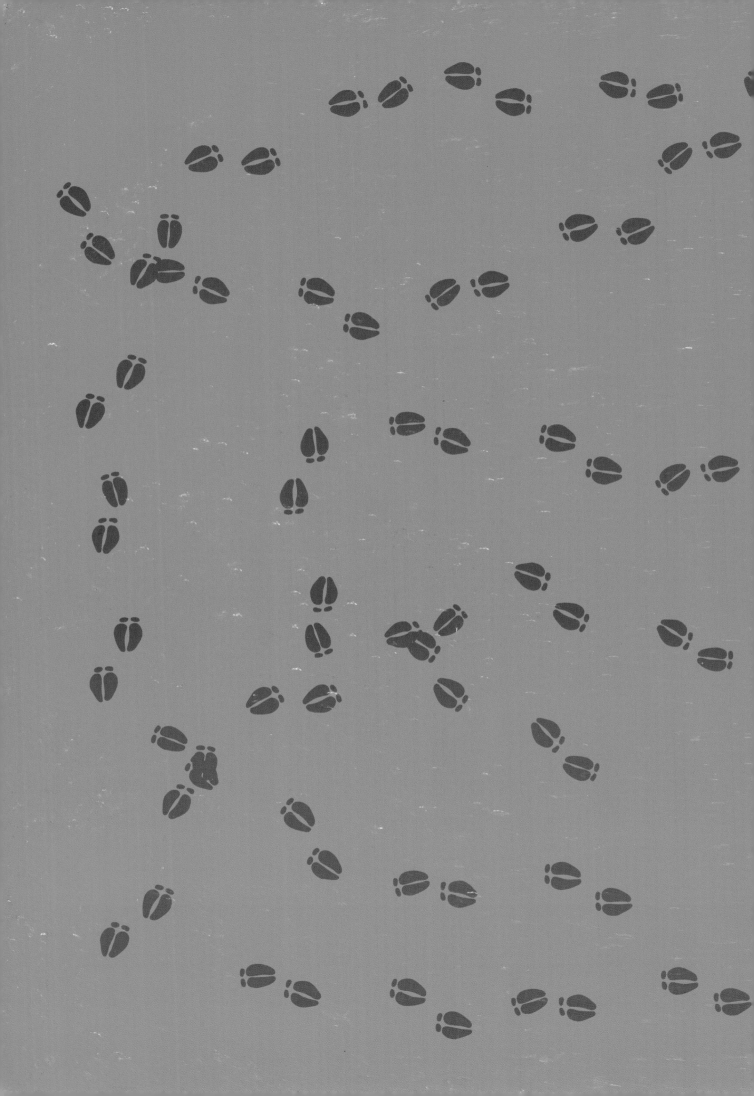